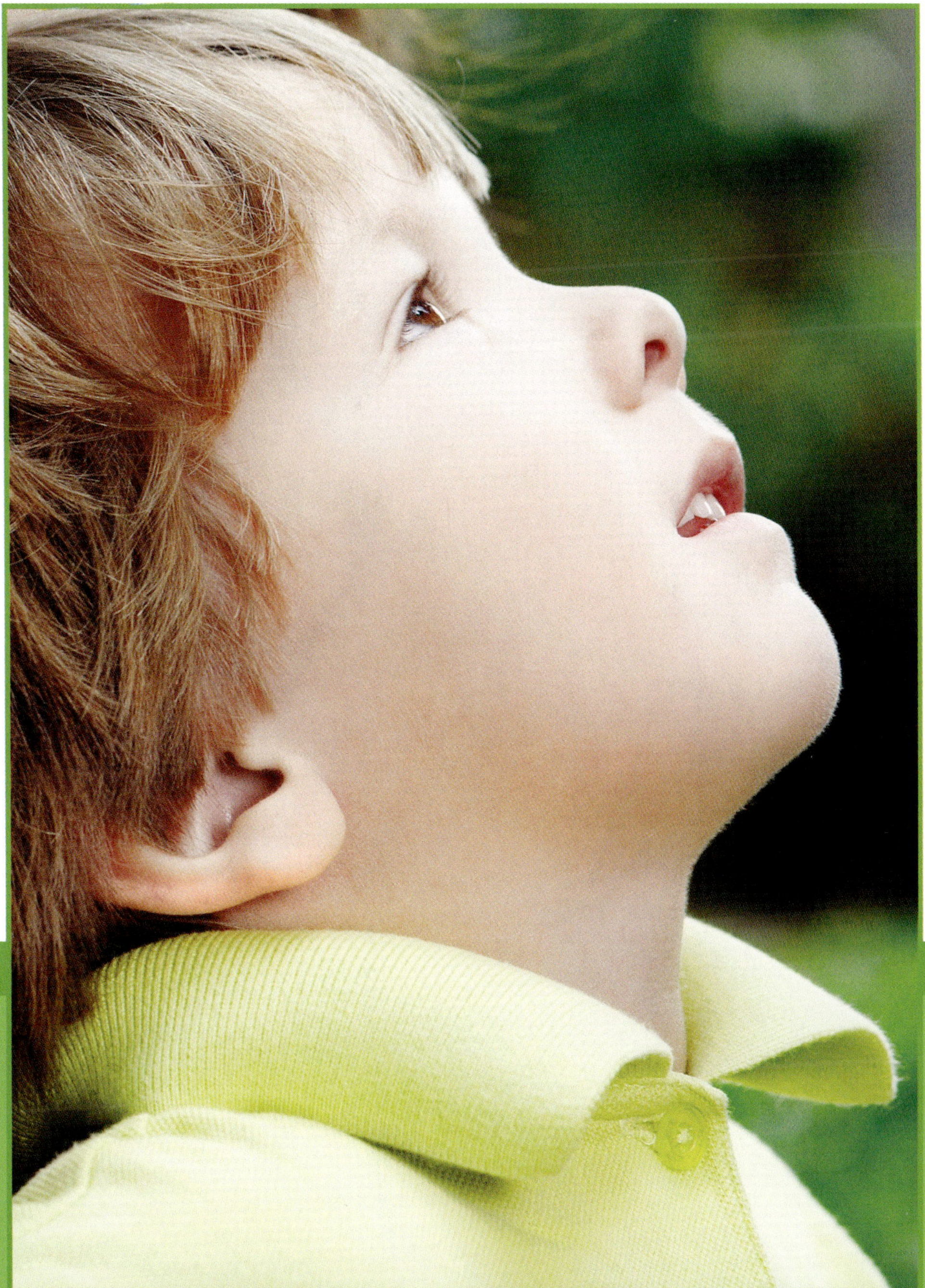

My Whole Self Before YOU

A Child's Prayer and Learning Guide Modeled after the Lord's Prayer

Susan Case Bonner

Traverse City, MI

© 2012, 2013 Susan Case Bonner. All rights reserved. All photos in this book are properly licensed. No part of this book may be reproduced or transmitted in any form or by any means, electronic or mechanical, including photocopying, recording, or by any information storage and retrieval system, without permission in writing from the publisher.

Published by Kid Niche Publishing, Traverse City, MI
www.kidniche.com

Publisher's Cataloging-Publication Data
Bonner, Susan Case.

My whole self before you : a child's prayer and learning guide modeled after the Lord's prayer /
Susan Case Bonner. – Traverse City, MI : Kid Niche Pub., 2012.

p. ; cm.

ISBN13: 978-0-9852712-0-6

1. Lord's prayer. 2. Children—Prayers and devotions. 3. Families—Religious life. 4. Children—Religious life. I. Title.

BV230.B66 2012

226.9606—dc22   2011941938

Project coordination by Jenkins Group, Inc.
www.BookPublishing.com

Cover and interior design: Eric Tufford
Manuscript Editor: Rebecca Chown
Biblical Editor: Dr. David R. Walls

Special thanks to Baseline United Methodist Church for permission to use their lovely stained glass windows as illustrations.
The actual windows are part of the old stone church building that houses this congregation between Battle Creek and Bellevue, Michigan.

A grateful nod to David Vandlen, the artist who created these windows
and to artist, Michael Novak, for recommending the stained glass window concept.

Ongoing thanks to my husband, Keith, for the contributions he has made in the form of supportive encouragement, ideas that were better than mine, and the gentle love he daily showers on me. Without his help, I would not be able to function as effectively in the world of creativity.

Printed in the United States by Worzalla Publishing, Second Printing, March 2013

17 16 15 14 13 • 6 5 4 3 2

Author's Note: The version of the Lord's Prayer used in this book (minus the doxology) is based on the wording that King Henry VIII established as the standard for all English speaking people in the sixteenth century before breaking ties with the Roman Catholic Church. It is patterned after William Tyndale's translation of 1525. All other Bible quotations are taken directly from the New American Standard Bible of 1971.

A Word to Parents and Teachers

Jesus said to them, "Permit the children to come to Me; do not hinder them; for the kingdom of God belongs to such as these." Mark 10:14

Young children want to talk to God. Parents want to help their children grow in this endeavor. But how do we as parents train our children to pray without inhibiting their God-given spontaneity and zeal? How do we help them go beyond the endless "Bless Aunt Ediths" without making prayer a lifeless list of do's and don'ts?

The answer lies in Jesus' response to his disciples' request, "Lord, teach us to pray." Instead of teaching them about prayer, Jesus taught his disciples a model prayer that became a tutorial for helping them understand how to approach God on any subject.

Applying this great teaching example, I wrote a prayer for my young daughter Katherine that blended Jesus' timeless concepts with her simple way of saying things. Although longer than a typical child's prayer, Katherine not only prayed the words with enthusiasm and meaning, she also memorized all the verses effortlessly. This prayer became the tangible framework for helping her grow in her understanding of who God is and how to talk to him.

Along with Katherine's prayer, this book includes a learning guide that outlines:

- the Bible truths taught in each verse of the prayer
- the Bible stories and passages that teach these truths
- a summary of the prayer life of Jesus

These lessons can be used as:

- bedtime readings
- a family devotional guide
- home school, Christian school, or church school curriculum

It is my sincere hope that this resource will be a Spirit-directed springboard launching your child into a lifetime of meaningful and effective conversations with God.

Susan Case Bonner

Dedication

To my daughter, Katherine,
whose pure and simple love for Jesus
inspired this prayer.

To my son, Justin,
whose tender heart and impish ways
reinforced the need for this prayer.

Dear Father
in heaven,

I come
and I bow

my whole self
before you.

Please hear me
right now.

I'm glad that you love me.

I'm glad that you care

for me and my family

and folks everywhere.

I'm glad you sent Jesus. I know he's your Son.

I'm learning about all the things he has done—

Like living

and dying

and living again,

so all who receive him may live up in heav'n.

I'd like to come see you, but 'til I can come,

please help me
to do things

as you want
them done.

Please help me show kindness to others, I pray.

Please keep
me from evil

and help
me obey.

Please give me those things, God,

you know
that I need,

but free me from

selfishness,
pouting,
and greed.

17

And for all the bad things

I say and I do,

forgive me and teach me

to be more like you.

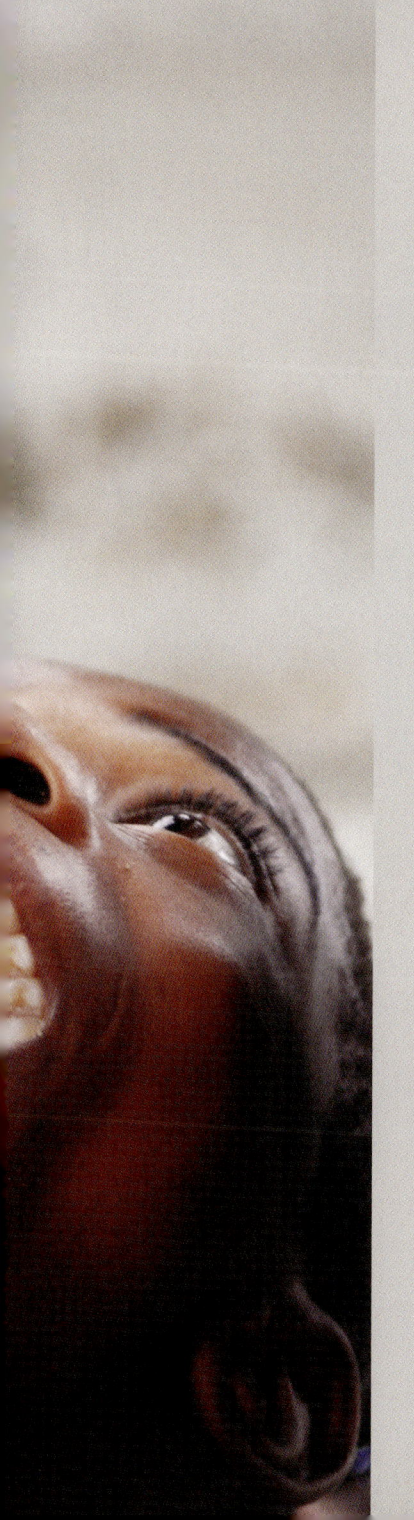

Thank you,
dear Father,

and

thank you
again—

to you be all glory forever.

Amen.

My Whole Self Before You

Dear Father in heaven, I come and I bow
my whole self before you. Please hear me right now.

I'm glad that you love me. I'm glad that you care
for me and my family and folks everywhere.

I'm glad you sent Jesus. I know he's your Son.
I'm learning about all the things he has done—

Like living and dying and living again,
so all who receive him may live up in heav'n.

I'd like to come see you, but 'til I can come,
please help me to do things as you want them done.

Please help me show kindness to others, I pray.
Please keep me from evil and help me obey.

Please give me those things, God, you know that I need,
but free me from selfishness, pouting, and greed.

And for all the bad things I say and I do,
forgive me and teach me to be more like you.

Thank you, dear Father, and thank you again—
to you be all glory forever. Amen.

Side by Side Comparison to the Lord's Prayer

The Lord's Prayer (Our Father)	My Whole Self Before YOU
Our Father who art in heaven,	Dear Father in heaven,
Hallowed be thy name.	I come and I bow my whole self before you.
Thy kingdom come. Thy will be done on earth as it is in heaven.	I'd like to come see you, but 'til I can come, please help me to do things as you want them done.
Give us this day our daily bread.	Please give me those things, God, you know that I need.
And forgive us our trespasses, as we forgive those who trespass against us.	And for all the bad things I say and I do, forgive me and teach me to be more like you.
And lead us not into temptation, but deliver us from evil.	Please keep me from evil and help me obey.
(Doxology) For Thine is the kingdom, and the power, and the glory forever. Amen.*	To you be all glory forever. Amen.

* "For Thine is the kingdom, and the power, and the glory forever. Amen" is a version of a song-like phrase early Christians recited as a praise ending to the Lord's Prayer. Whether it was part of the original prayer Jesus taught his followers is questioned, because it is not found in the earliest manuscripts of the book of Matthew. This short verse of praise is called a doxology and is based on I Chronicles 29:11.

The Learning Guide

The Learning Guide

Now that you have read the prayer, it is time to help your child learn the biblical truths and passages upon which the prayer is based. This is how the guide is set up:

1. Each of the nine verses of the prayer is illustrated with a stained glass window.

2. Following each illustrated verse are the highlighted Bible truths taught within that verse.

3. Following each Bible truth is a list of the Bible passages that teach it. These are numbered as lessons.

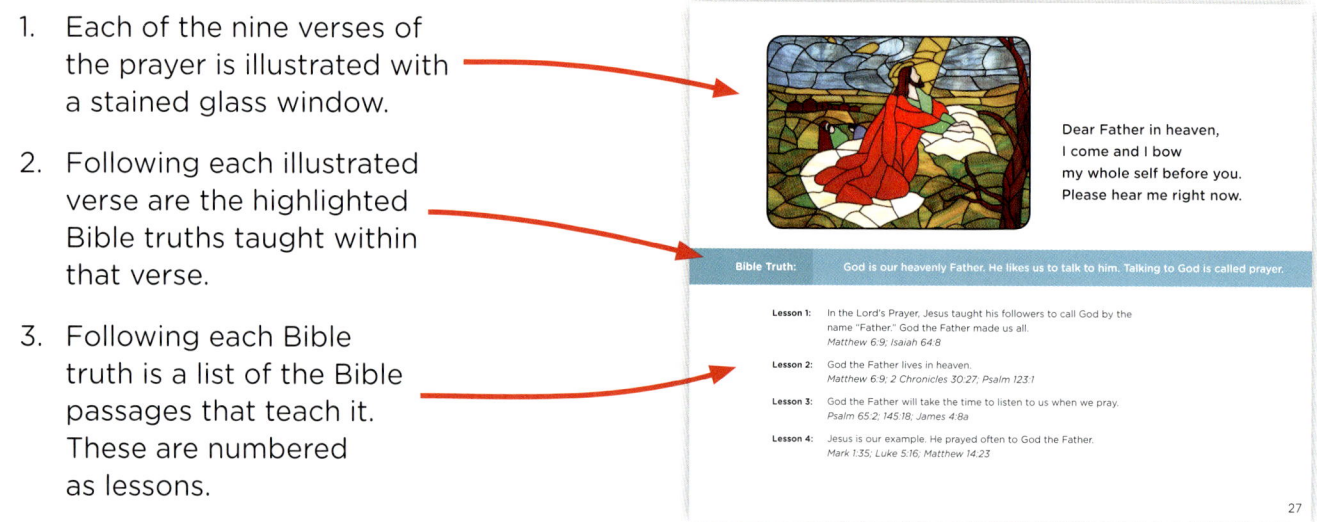

This is how to use the learning guide:

- Read and talk about a lesson with your child.
- Then, repeat the words of that lesson's prayer-verse a few times with your child.
- Next, pray the entire prayer to God along with your child as you leaf through the pictures in the front of the book (personal P.S.'s at the end are good).
- Combine or omit lessons according to your child's individual needs and maturity level. By the time you complete all the lessons, your child will have effortlessly memorized the entire prayer.

A few recommendations:

- Read each lesson in advance. Also, take the time to read about the prayer life of Jesus on pages 42–43.
- Use simple visuals with the Bible stories whenever possible—an object, some stick figures, a facial expression. And don't forget the effectiveness of the other four senses or a probing question.
- Keep a brief diary, because you will want to remember the great insights your child shares with you and the answers to prayer you experience together.

Dear Father in heaven,
I come and I bow
my whole self before you.
Please hear me right now.

Bible Truth: God is our heavenly Father. He likes us to talk to him. Talking to God is called prayer.

Lesson 1: In the Lord's Prayer, Jesus taught his followers to call God by the name "Father." God the Father made us all.
Matthew 6:9; Isaiah 64:8

Lesson 2: God the Father lives in heaven.
Matthew 6:9; 2 Chronicles 30:27; Psalm 123:1

Lesson 3: God the Father will take the time to listen to us when we pray.
Psalm 65:2; 145:18; James 4:8a

Lesson 4: Jesus is our example. He prayed often to God the Father.
Mark 1:35; Luke 5:16; Matthew 14:23

Bible Truth: God is pleased and honored when we treat him with respect and come to him humbly.

Lesson 5: In the Lord's Prayer, Jesus taught that God's name is to be hallowed.
Matthew 6:9

> "Hallowed" means that we are to treat God and his name with great respect and love.
> "Humbly" means lowly. Since God is much greater than we are, we are to treat him as our king.

The next four Bible stories help us better understand the words "hallowed" and "humble":

Lesson 6: God showed his greatness to Isaiah.
Isaiah 6:1–8

Lesson 7: The parable of the Pharisee and the tax collector.
Luke 18:9–14; James 4:6

> A "parable" is a short, simple story about everyday things that teaches a heavenly lesson.
> It helps us better understand the way God sees things.

Lesson 8: Peter's unexpected catch of fish.
Luke 5:1–11

Lesson 9: The weeping woman and the parable of the two borrowers.
Luke 7:36–50

I'm glad that you love me.
I'm glad that you care
for me and my family
and folks everywhere.

| **Bible Truth:** | **God loves and cares for all people.** |

Lesson 10: God deeply loves all people of the world. He welcomes people of every race to trust and obey him.
John 3:16; Acts 10:34–35

Lesson 11: God shows kindness to both good and evil people.
Matthew 5:44–45

Lesson 12: God loves children.
Mark 10:13–16

Lesson 13: God knows even the smallest details about us and highly values us.
Luke 12:6–7

Lesson 14: No one is too bad for God to love.
Luke 15:1–32 (The parable of the lost things)

I'm glad you sent Jesus.
I know he's your Son.
I'm learning about all
the things he has done—

Bible Truth:	Jesus is God the Son. He became a man so that he could teach people what God is like, show people how to live, and save people from death that lasts forever.

Lesson 15: Jesus was born. *Luke 2:1–20*

Lesson 16: Jesus grew as a boy. *Luke 2:40-52*

Lesson 17: Jesus was baptized by John. *Matthew 3:1–6, 13–17*

Lesson 18: Jesus was tempted by Satan. *Matthew 4:1–11*

Lesson 19: Jesus was an amazing teacher. *Luke 4:14–15, 31–37; John 7:14–16*

Lesson 20: Jesus forgave and healed people. *Luke 5:17–26; Matthew 12:9–14*

Lesson 21: Jesus trained his disciples. *Mark 1:14–20; Luke 5:27–32; 6:12–19; 8:1–3; 9:1–2*

Lesson 22: Jesus taught his disciples about faith. *Mark 4:35–41; John 6:1–15; Matthew 14:22–33*

Lesson 23: Jesus did awesome miracles. *Mark 5:21-43*

Lesson 24: Jesus showed his God-look (glory) and freed a boy from a demon. *Mark 9:2-10, 14-29*

Lesson 25: Jesus raised a dead man back to life. *John 11:1-48, 53*

"Pharisees" were members of a religious group in Israel that oversaw the synagogues and schools. They were often middle class businessmen who assisted the scribes (teachers of the Law known as rabbis). They believed that every detail of the Old Testament Law was important to obey, even the spoken rules that had been added and passed down from one teacher to another. For example: spitting on a rock is all right on the Sabbath (the day of rest), but it is not okay to spit on the ground, because that might move dirt, which would be considered work. Some of the Pharisees respected Rabbi Jesus and followed his teachings, but many saw him as a threat to their way of thinking and wanted to get rid of him.

"Sadducees" were members of another religious group that oversaw the Temple in Jerusalem. They were important priests from rich families who controlled the ruling council. Jesus and his teachings were a threat to their power.

Lesson 26: Jesus saw into people's hearts—both good and bad. *Mark 12:41-44; Luke 20:19-26*

Lesson 27: Jesus was betrayed and arrested. *Matthew 26:14-16; Luke 22:39-54*

Lesson 28: Jesus was put on trial. *Luke 22:63-71; Mark 15:1-15*

Lesson 29: Jesus was put to death on a cross. *Mark 15:16-47*

Lesson 30: Jesus came back to life. *John 20:1-31*

Lesson 31: Jesus returned to heaven to live with God the Father. *Mark 16:19; Acts 1:9-11*

Lesson 32: Jesus will come back to rule the world. *Mark 14:61-62; Revelation 1:7; Daniel 7:13-14*

Like living and dying
and living again,
so all who receive him
may live up in heav'n.

Bible Truth:	Anyone who receives Jesus as God and Savior becomes God's child and will live with him in heaven when he dies.

"Receiving" is the same thing as believing.

Lesson 33: Some people rejected Jesus when he lived on earth. They did not receive him or believe that he was God the Son. But anyone who did receive him became God's child. *John 1:11–12*

Lesson 34: God's Son, Jesus, became a human being and died to save people from their sins. Everyone who believes this gets to live forever with God. *Matthew 1:18–21; John 1:28–29, 32–34; 3:16*

Lesson 35: Jesus is making a city in heaven where believing people will live with him forever. It is a happier and more beautiful place than anyone can ever imagine. *John 14:1–3; Revelation 21:1–4, 18, 21, 27; 22:1–5*

Lesson 36: A criminal believed in Jesus and went to live with him in heaven. *Luke 23:33–43*

I'd like to come see you,
but 'til I can come,
please help me to do things
as you want them done.

Bible Truth: God wants us to live for him and choose to do things the way he would do them.

Lesson 37: In the Lord's Prayer, Jesus taught his followers to pray these words: "Thy kingdom come, thy will be done on earth as it is in heaven." *Matthew 6:10*

The following Bible stories help us understand what it means to do God's will:

Lesson 38: We are to seek God first above all other things. *Matthew 6:19–21, 25–33*

Lesson 39: We are to act wisely by doing what Jesus teaches. *Matthew 7:21, 24–27**

Lesson 40: Beware! We are not to live only for possessions and pleasure. *Luke 12:15–21**

Lesson 41: We are to use what God gives us to do good. *Matthew 25:14–30**

Lesson 42: We are to serve other people and meet their needs. *Matthew 25:31–46*

*These stories are parables.

Please help me show kindness to others, I pray. Please keep me from evil and help me obey.

Bible Truth:	**God wants us to love and serve other people.**

Lesson 43: The two greatest commandments. *Mark 12:28-31*

Lesson 44: Be like God: love everyone, even those who hate you. *Luke 6:27-36; 23:33-34*

Lesson 45: Be like Jesus: serve other people and put their needs first. *Mark 10:35-37, 41-45; John 13:3-5, 12-15; Philippians 2:3-8*

Lesson 46: The parable of the good Samaritan. *Luke 10:25-37*

Bible Truth:	**God wants us to do good, not evil, and to obey him.**

Lesson 47: In the Lord's Prayer, Jesus taught his followers to pray these words: "Lead us not into temptation, but deliver us from evil." *Matthew 6:13*

Lesson 48: When we are tempted, we desire to do something that is not good. *James 1:13-14; Hebrews 4:15-16; I Corinthians 10:13*

Obeying is hard, at times, because we don't always want to do what is good. Sometimes we even want to do what we know we shouldn't do. When this happens, we are being tempted. God does not send temptations to us, but neither does he stop these intense thoughts and desires from coming. Why? Because he wants us to grow strong inside. If he controlled our thoughts and desires, we would never learn to say "no" for ourselves, and that is a very important part of growing up. God totally understands how hard it is to say "no," because Jesus was also tempted; therefore, he offers us help if we ask him for it. He gives us wisdom and strength as we face a temptation, forgiveness if we fail, and blessing when we succeed. And he promises that if we hang on, he will show us how to escape from a temptation, because he doesn't want us to give up—he just wants us to grow. (See James 1:2-4)

The following Commandments explain what God means by "good."*

Lesson 49: Worship the one true God only and put him first. *Exodus 20:1-6*

Lesson 50: Don't use God's name in a disrespectful or meaningless way. *Exodus 20:7*

Lesson 51: Take a special day of rest each week. *Exodus 20:8-11*

Lesson 52: Honor and obey your parents. *Exodus 20:12; Ephesians 6:1-4*

Lesson 53: Don't murder or even hate. *Exodus 20:13; Matthew 5:21-24*

Lesson 54: Be faithful to your marriage partner. *Exodus 20:14*

Lesson 55: Don't steal. *Exodus 20:15*

Lesson 56: Don't say things that are not true about other people. *Exodus 20:16*

Lesson 57: Don't be jealous of, or desire, or take what belongs to others. *Exodus 20:17*

*Lessons 49-57 are known as the Ten Commandments. Some Christians separate the first commandment into two and others separate the last commandment into two.

Bible Truth: Obeying is about doing, not just about hearing or knowing.

Lesson 58: In the parable of the two sons, which one obeyed?
Matthew 21:28-32

Lesson 59: Hearing and knowing are different than doing.
James 1:22-25

Please give me those things, God, you know that I need, but free me from selfishness, pouting, and greed.

| **Bible Truth:** | God wants us to depend on him for the things we need each day by asking him for them. |

Lesson 60: In the Lord's Prayer, Jesus taught his followers to pray these words: "Give us this day our daily bread." *Matthew 6:11*

Lesson 61: God gives good things to those who ask.
Matthew 7:7-11; Lamentations 3:25; Psalm 37:4; James 4:3

Lesson 62: God gives a calm heart to those who pray about their worries and give thanks.
Philippians 4:4-7

Lesson 63: God gives wisdom (good sense) to those who ask him for it.
James 1:5-8

Lesson 64: God guides those who trust him.
Proverbs 3:5-6

Bible Truth: No one needs to teach us to be selfish and do wrong things. We are all born that way. It is what comes naturally. God, the Holy Spirit, is the one who helps us to be loving, cheerful, and generous rather than selfish, pouty, and greedy.

Lesson 65: Every day, there is a tug of war going on inside our hearts between the Holy Spirit and our selfish, natural desires. The Holy Spirit urges us to do what pleases God, while our natural desires urge us to do what is selfish.
Galatians 5:16–17

Lesson 66: We don't have to do what our selfish, natural desires want us to do. We can say "no" to these desires by choosing to do what is good. This is the freedom that Jesus gives us.
Galatians 5:1; Ephesians 4:30–32

Lesson 67: Beware! Our selfish, natural desires pop up and start pulling at times when we least expect them. Don't give in to them. Instead, keep choosing to do what pleases God and he will reward you.
Galatians 6:7–9

And for all the bad things
I say and I do,
forgive me and teach me
to be more like you.

Bible Truth: God wants us to tell him when we do wrong things and ask him for forgiveness. He is faithful to forgive our sins as long as we also forgive other people for theirs.

Lesson 68: In the Lord's Prayer, Jesus taught his followers to pray these words: "Forgive us our trespasses (or "debts"), as we forgive those who trespass against us" (or "as we forgive our debtors"). *Matthew 6:12, 14–15*

Some Bible translations use the word "trespasses" and others use the word "debts." A "trespass" is a turning away from what is right and true. A "debt" is a wrong that needs forgiveness and repair.

Lesson 69: God forgives us when we tell him we have sinned. *I John 1:8–10; Psalm 86:5*

Lesson 70: Zaccheus turned away from his sin and Jesus forgave him. *Luke 19:1–10*

Lesson 71: The parable of the unforgiving servant. *Matthew 18:21–35*

Bible Truth: When Jesus returned to heaven, he sent God, the Holy Spirit, to take his place as our teacher.

Lesson 72: The Holy Spirit loves and reaches out to all people. *John 16:8–11*

    1) He convinces people of their sin and leads them to Jesus.

    2) He encourages people to do what is right.

    3) He reminds people that one day they will have to explain their lives to God.

Lesson 73: The Holy Spirit lives inside those of us who believe in Jesus. *John 14:16–17*

Lesson 74: 1) He guides us to understand truth. *John 16:13*

Lesson 75: 2) He helps us to live in a way that is pleasing to God. *Galatians 5:16, 22–23*

Lesson 76: 3) He tells the Father our heart-words when we don't know what words to pray. *Romans 8:26*

Lesson 77: 4) He prays for us himself as a defender and a friend. *Romans 8:27*

Thank you, dear Father, and thank you again— to you be all glory forever. Amen.

Bible Truth:	God the Father is delighted when we take the time to praise and thank him for who he is and what he has done for us. This is called worship or giving glory to God.

Lesson 78: Angels and shepherds gave glory and praise to God. *Luke 2:8-20*

Lesson 79: A leper and a blind man gave glory and thanks to God. *Luke 17:11-19; 18:35-43*

Lesson 80: Every being is to bless and praise the Lord. *Psalm 72:18-19; 150:6*

"Glory" is fame and honor that are highly deserved (because of excellent character and actions). In other words, God deserves the spotlight because he is so awesome! When we tell God how wonderful he is and thank him for all he has done for us, it is like shining a big spotlight of praise on him and saying, "Father, you are great!" This brings glory to God.

After that, all there is to say is "Amen." Amen means "so be it" or "truly."

The Prayer Life of Jesus

The Prayer Life of Jesus
A Biblical Resource for Parents and Teachers

JESUS IS OUR EXAMPLE. He prayed often to God the Father, at different times, in different places, and for different reasons. He talked, cried, questioned, thanked, praised, requested, and interceded to God with faith, energy, emotion, and honesty. The following passages from the four gospels give us a glimpse into the prayer life of Jesus:

1. **Matthew 4:1-11** Before beginning his three-year public ministry—to be prepared for the temptations that would come with power and fame—Jesus fasted and prayed for forty days in the wilderness (desert).

2. **Luke 6:12-13** Before choosing the group of twelve disciples he would personally train, Jesus prayed all night at "the mountain."

3. **Mark 1:32-39** Before continuing his preaching and healing ministry—to be sure he was doing what God wanted and going where God wanted—Jesus left his companions early in the morning before it was light and went to a solitary (lonely) place to pray.

4. **Luke 5:16; 22:39-41** Jesus prayed regularly and often in places away from the crowds, such as at the Mount of Olives and in the wilderness.

5. **Matthew 11:25-27** After rebuking the greater population of Galilee for remaining spiritually unchanged even though they had seen amazing miracles, Jesus praised God the Father that by his design spiritual truth is only understood by people with teachable hearts.

6. **Luke 9:28; 11:1** At times, Jesus took his disciples with him when he prayed. After seeing Jesus pray "in a certain place," one of his disciples asked him to teach them to pray.

7. **John 11:38-44** Before bringing Lazarus back to life—so that those who were watching would know and believe that his power came from God—Jesus thanked God the Father for what was about to happen in the hearing of the Jewish mourners outside the cave tomb in the village of Bethany.

8. **John 12:20-30** While foretelling his death to his disciples in the midst of a multitude of people, Jesus prayed, "Father, glorify Thy name." For the benefit of those listening, including some non-Jews, God the Father answered from heaven in an audible voice, "I have both glorified it, and will glorify it again." This took place during the Passover Feast after Jesus' triumphal entry into Jerusalem.

9. **Mark 14:22-23** Before eating and drinking the Passover bread and wine at the Last Supper, Jesus gave thanks to God in the Upper Room in Jerusalem. (See also John 6:11)

10. **Luke 22:31-32** Because of Satan's attempts to destroy their faith, Jesus prayed for his disciples by name, asking God to preserve and strengthen their faith.

11. **Matthew 26:36-46; Mark 14:32-42; Luke 22:39-46; John 17:1-26** Before allowing the Jews to arrest him, Jesus went to the Garden of Gethsemane on the Mount of Olives to pray:

<ol style="list-style-type: lower-alpha">
<li>for the courage to die as God the Father had planned,</li>
<li>that God the Father would allow Jesus' godhood (glory) to be revealed through his death and resurrection,</li>
<li>that God would strengthen and unite his followers after his death and resurrection,</li>
<li>that God would keep his followers loyal and protect them from following Satan's lies,</li>
<li>that God would empower his followers to increasingly obey the truth and live pure lives,</li>
<li>that the world would understand who Jesus is and why he came as a result of seeing the love and unity of his followers, and</li>
<li>that God would grant these requests not only for his present followers but also for those who would believe in the future.</li>
</ol>

12. **Luke 23:33-34** While dying on the cross at Golgotha, an area outside Jerusalem, Jesus asked God the Father to forgive those who crucified him, because they did not know what they were doing.

13. **Matthew 27:46; Mark 15:34; Luke 23:46** At the ninth hour (3:00 p.m.), Jesus cried out in agony as he experienced total abandonment and separation from God. Just before taking his last breath, Jesus cried out again to God saying, "Father, into Thy hands I commit My spirit."

14. **See also Hebrews 5:7-8 and Philippians 2:5-11.**

IN SUMMARY:

For himself, Jesus prayed for:
- faithfulness
- loyalty
- insight
- direction
- focus
- perseverance
- courage
- selflessness
- obedience
- success of mission

For his followers, Jesus prayed for:
- faith
- strength
- unity
- loyalty
- protection from deceit
- power to increasingly obey God
- love

For the world, Jesus prayed for:
- understanding of who he is and why he came
- forgiveness and mercy

Jesus thanked and praised God for:
- listening to him and granting his request
- revealing truth only to those who, like children, are open and teachable

A Closing Word of Encouragement

It is my hope that the words and concepts of this book strongly reinforce the truth that talking to God is a skill that matters. As with any skill, the more we practice, the more we grow in confidence. So let's pray often. Let's pray with meaning. Let's pray with teachable hearts and expect great things from God. May the heartfelt commitment of Psalm 116:1–2 be true in each of our lives:

"I love the Lord, because He hears my voice and my supplications. Because He has inclined His ear to me, therefore I shall call upon Him as long as I live."

I shall teach my children to do the same.

With love for you and yours,

Susan Case Bonner

Susan Case Bonner graduated from Columbia International University in Columbia, South Carolina, with a bachelor's degree in Biblical Education. As a Christian school teacher, home school teacher, Christian education director, Sunday school teacher, chapel and conference speaker, and parent of two children, she has dedicated the last thirty-five years of her life to teaching the Bible simply and creatively so that children of all ages can understand and embrace its teachings.

Susan currently writes and publishes children's books in Traverse City, Michigan, with her husband Keith. She is actively involved in her home church and enjoys interior design, thrift shopping, and antiquing.

Companion student workbooks are available at www.kidniche.com.